THE COUNTRIES WE LIVE IN

OTHER BOOKS BY PETER EVERWINE

In the House of Light
(1970)

Collecting the Animals
(1973)

Keeping the Night
(1977)

The Static Element: Selected Poems of Natan Zach
(1982)

Figures Made Visible in the Sadness of Time
(2003)

Speaking of Accidents
(2003)

From the Meadow: Selected and New Poems
(2004)

What a Word Dreamt
(2005)

Working the Song Fields: Poems from the Aztecs
(2010)

Traces
(2010)

THE COUNTRIES WE LIVE IN

SELECTED POEMS **NATAN ZACH** 1955-1979

TRANSLATED BY PETER EVERWINE

TAVERN BOOKS

Portland & Salt Lake City

Printed in the United States of America

Cover art: Cecilia Yang, *Two Locusts*, 2011. Ink drawing.
Copyright ©Cecilia Yang. Courtesy of the artist.

Zach, Natan, 1930-
Everwine, Peter, 1930-

ISBN-13: 978-1-935635-08-6
ISBN-10: 1-935635-08-5

Earlier versions of these translations were published in
The Static Element: Selected Poems of Natan Zach
(Atheneum, 1982)

FIRST EDITION

98765432 First Printing

TAVERN BOOKS
Portland & Salt Lake City
www.tavernbooks.com

CONTENTS

from ALL THE MILK AND THE HONEY (1964)

from NORTH EASTERLY (1979)

NOTE TO THE NEW EDITION

The book you hold in your hand is a revised and expanded edition of *The Static Element: Selected Poems of Natan Zach*, published by Atheneum in 1982 and now out of print. A translator seldom has the opportunity to enter anew the work of some thirty years ago. The experience is humbling. I can only express my gratitude to Michael McGriff and Carl Adamshick, publishers of Tavern Books, for the opportunity to bring Natan Zach's poetry to a new generation of readers.

For this edition I have added poems previously unpublished in English, revised others that now seem flawed, for one reason or another, added end notes to clarify important allusions, and given the book a new title: *The Countries We Live In: Selected Poems of Natan Zach, 1955-1979*—a title that now seems more in keeping with the entire collection. I have left unchanged my preface to the Atheneum edition.

Zach, at the age of eighty, is Israel's foremost living poet and has been honored throughout Europe. Obviously a extensive body of work exists beyond the early poems found in *The Countries We Live In*, and Zach is due for a volume of selected poems in English that will adequately represent his long career. In the meantime, here is the work that established him as a major force in the modernist movement in Israeli poetry.

I am again indebted to my colleague Shulamit Yasny-Starkman, who has gone through the poems—old and new—with her usual care, insight, and advice. The final responsibility, however, is mine.

Peter Everwine
Fresno, CA 2010

BIOGRAPHICAL NOTE

Born in Berlin in 1930, Natan Zach immigrated with his family to Israel (then Palestine) in 1935. One of Israel's most distinguished poets, as well as a writer of influential essays, he has been described by Shimon Sandbank as "the most articulate and insistent spokesman" of the modernist movement in Hebrew poetry.

Following the publication of his first two books, *First Poems* (1955) and *Various Poems* (1960), he was closely associated with Israeli theater until 1967. His third book, *All the Milk and the Honey*, was published in 1964.

After 1968 he settled in Britain where he completed a doctorate from the University of Essex and worked as the London news editor for the Jewish Telegraphic Agency. He returned to Israel in 1979 and taught at the University of Haifa. That same year he published *North-Easterly*, a collection of poems. Later books include *Hard to Remember* (1984), *Because I'm Around* (1996) and *For Man is a Tree of the Field* (1999).

Zach won the Bialik Prize for poetry in 1981, the Feronia Prize (Italy) in 1993 and the Israel Prize in 1995. His most recent prize, given for his *Collected Poems*, is the ACUM Prize in 2003. He has also written a literary autobiography, *From Year to Year It* (2010).

PREFACE TO THE 1982 EDITION

The poems of Natan Zach share something of the astringent style that has become familiar in the distressed literature of post-war modernism. Having been subjected to extraordinary historical pressures, they are guarded in tone, oblique, frequently satiric and pointed with wit, deliberatively reductive. "It's the salt in me that talks," Zach says in one of his poems, a distillation clearly antidotal to the overtly national and ideological poetry that, in his words, had satisfied "a previous generation's thirst for grand certainties." There are few certainties, grand or otherwise, to hold fast to in his work. To follow the movement of a Zach poem is to follow a nervous and analytical intelligence that refuses to be taken in by conventions of sentiment or piety. A tenacious ironist, deeply aware of human isolation and the elaborate illusions we construct as our refuges (the refuge of poetry included), his characteristic attitude is "Be careful...Don't expect." His reticence becomes a way of holding things in check, an integrity that is both a literary position and a personal response to experience.

Zach is a difficult poet to translate. He can be the sparest and most colloquial of poets, but he also exploits fully the unique character of Hebrew—that ancient language "torn from its sleep in the Bible" (Yehuda Amichai) and revived to the demands of a changed world. Like other Israeli poets, he moves easily among biblical and liturgical referents, but he is innovative in the way he rapidly juxtaposes various linguistic levels. Biblical phrase is set against flat banality; hyperbole is set against laconic understatement or the lingo of the streets. Thus he exploits language and also subjects it to implicit criticism, attacking fashion and cant. Essentially a dramatic poet, his conversational rhythms are equally complex in counterpoint, and he often uses rhyme—especially internal rhyme—as a device to cancel or counterbalance statements of excessive intensity or pomposity. The effect is frequently one of restless improvisation and tension, and it is a music and a texture of meaning that a translator can only attempt to approximate. A flat literal version is certain to drain him of major effects.

A case in point: I once showed to Zach an early version of "Failure," feeling quite smug in having captured—or so I believed—a rather plaintive tone in a poem that spoke quietly of the persistence of desire and its inevitable failure. Zach was horrified. I had "softened" his poem considerably, accurately catching its literal meaning but failing to consider the function of his abrupt rhymes and shifts in idiom. I had lost the proper distancing of his irony. My version spoke of pathos; his poem articulated a judgment. So much for tender-mindedness.

This difficulty is somewhat diminished in Zach's most recent work. In what seems to be an effort to accommodate a broader range of materials and "to speak to the moment, like a journalist," he has loosened his forms considerably. As he says, in "The Problem," the poet must find a form that is

> like a diamond, but also like an ample bed
> where a man can stretch without
> knocking his head against a wall,
> and like a taut string
> with no corners to catch dust.

These paradoxical demands seem characteristic of the tensions in Zach's work. Never a comfortable poet, he reminds us that a poem is an ambiguous system of insights, "a static element" addressed to the immediacy of the moment and engaged in the daily coming and going of our perplexed lives. Shaped by the artificer's traditional cunning, it is like an intricately fashioned net in which the rare and the redeemable may yet be surprised, "here and there,/blossoming," It is not a poetry of optimism or easy affirmation, but at times there rises a guarded belief that

There is something in promises—
remote, a secret wrapped in desires
no one can unravel—
the wadi winding its way,
the city that rose from salt,
the strange end of Job:
forms of things to come.
["A Gust of Warm Wind"]

A guarded belief, not a cause for celebration. As Zach says,

A starry night?
No. Not yet.
["On the Impossibility of the Unromantic Condition"]

Despite Zach's stature as a poet and his importance to the development of Hebrew poetry, he is virtually unknown to an English-speaking audience. A slim pamphlet of his poems, translated by the poet Jon Silkin, appeared in England under the title *Against Parting* (Northern House, 1967), but this has not been easily available. What thus began as my own effort to read and understand his work has evolved over the years into this present collection.

The translations that follow are drawn from Zach's published volumes to date, with the exception of his Italian travel poems. The order of poems in each section is my own. A number of poems I wanted to include had to be abandoned; my English was not adequate to their demands.

As for the method of translation: I worked from literal cribs, glosses, and notes prepared by Shulamit Yasny-Starkman, a native Israeli. Each version was then subjected to critical discussion and subsequent revisions. The final result, therefore, has been a true collaboration, although the responsibility for any deficiencies must be mine alone. I am aware that this method leaves much to be desired. My purpose here is not to defend it but simply to acknowledge it. Within the limits of my understanding and my ability, my intention was to provide a clear sense of Zach's rigorous and unique poetry.

I am indebted to a number of friends who read versions of the manuscript and gave me the benefit of their critical insights, especially to Bill Broder, Philip Levine, and Robert Mezey.

I am especially grateful to Natan Zach for his hospitality,

his valuable comments, and his cooperation throughout this project. More than this, his support carried me through those times when I believed that no man in his right mind would undertake the task of translation.

Finally, I am pleased to acknowledge a long-standing debt of gratitude to Harry Ford.

Peter Everwine
[1982]

THE COUNTRIES WE LIVE IN

from FIRST POEMS
(1955)

BE CAREFUL

Be careful. Open your life
only to the wind that has touched distance.
Suffer the absent. Speak up
only in the nights of solitude. Know the day,
the fixed season, the moment,
and don't beg. Pay attention to what is still. Learn to bless
the shadow just beneath the skin. Don't
hide in words. Sit with the counsel of worms,
the wisdom of the maggot. Don't expect.

THE GOLD OF OPHIR

They unloaded the gold of Ophir
in the harbor.
A band was playing
beyond the shutters.
And I knew it was forbidden.
Forbidden.
In fifteen years,
or thirty,
or forty-five—
perhaps only then
I'll lie, like this,
in the dark room,
undressed,
silent,
when they unload the gold.

TO A STUDENT IN JERUSALEM

After ten steep, iron steps,
the small, stifling room, and higher still
a hot splinter of a moon plunged
into ashen clouds. In between,
a sticky light as if smeared on walls
by a *hamsin* wind too listless to stir
the laundry hanging from the tenements.

The echo of each movement returns you
to yourself—vague silhouette—as to a lullaby.
You remember and accept again
the body on the chair, head leaning
on the table, a finger
in the dust of darkness.

This is the breathing space between one solitude
and another, an oppressive reading
in a book that recedes from you—from this
momentary rest between demand
and release—moving out
into the open night

that knows you instantly by your hesitations.

A FINAL PARTING

When my girl walked out,
I put on my new suit
and went to a coffee shop.
Inside were three men:
a thin one, a fat
one, and one bald on top.
The fat one had a red rose
pinned to his coat.
When I entered and they saw me,
up jumped the bald one
and said, "Buddy, what's done
is done!"

A HAMSIN NIGHT

Even a stone in the wall will cry out—
if it hasn't cried out by now.
A city will break into song—
if it hasn't sung by now.
A tourist in the hotel. A pregnant woman.
A field-grade officer.

Wind will go down to the sea—
if it hasn't gone down by now.
A lithe body will stir the blood.
A woman from yesterday. A map of sand.
One person to another.

The landscape loses its name—
if it hasn't lost it by now.
Dust in the street turns back
into sand, as it was before.
A hundred dollar bill. A painted door.
Alone.

ALSO

Also a kind of bribery in loneliness
Also a kind of fraud in solitude
Also a kind of repression in sadness
Also a kind of oppression in keeping removed

There's a deep root that grows nothing
There's a secret cup of gall that sweetens

I SAW A WHITE BIRD

I saw a white bird in a black night
and I knew it wouldn't be long before the light
of my eyes would vanish in a black night.

I saw a cloud as small as a man's hand
and I knew, the first rain gusting in the wind,
I've failed to make anyone understand.

I saw a leaf that fell, a leaf falling.
Time is short. I am not complaining.

from VARIOUS POEMS
(1960)

WHEN GOD FIRST SAID

When God first said Let there be light
He meant it would not be dark for Him.
In that moment He didn't think about the sky,
but the trees were already filling with water,
the birds receiving air and body.
Then the first wind touched God's eyes
and He saw it in all His splendor
and thought It is good. He didn't think then
about people, people in their multitudes,
but they were already standing apart from the fig leaves,
unraveling in their hearts
a scheme about pain.
When God first thought of night
He didn't think about sleep.
So be it, God said, I will be happy.
But they were multitudes.

IN THE END

I've had enough! said the old man
and carefully shut the gate
behind him.

The boy, barely visible,
was growing smaller
at the end of the alley.

Everything goes! said the old man,
pain has its way in the end.
He turned and slept then.

And only one little finger, dreaming
of the world beyond the door,
whispered to itself, I want more!

But the cockroach in the cupboard spat
and said in its bitter tongue,
That's that!

A FINAL PARTING (LATER)

When my girl walked out
—so I once wrote—
I went to a coffee shop.
Inside were three men:
a thin one, a fat
one, and one bald on top.
The fat one had a rose...
remember that red rose
pinned to the coat

of the fat one (but not
of the bald one)?
Actually,
when I entered they never looked up.
A moment like this arrives:

One man enters and sits down
while another thinks
it was the wind opening the door.

Or perhaps not even that.

NOTHING

Nothing comes.
The night wind stirs its darkness
like night wind stirring darkness.
Nothing comes.

Nothing comes.
The door that was closed and opened
opened and closed.
Nothing comes.

Nothing comes.
Legs crossed, lamp on the table,
a shadow and an undershirt.
The one who entered is the one who left.
Nothing comes.

CHIEF MINISTER WORM

Chief Minster Worm, forgive me
if I have not respected your sisters,
the First Under-Secretary and the Second.

I had fully intended to do so,
but the firefly, you know, the firefly
left me with less than half my desire in hand.

I hope to carry out my plan tonight;
there may not come another time
when I feel such confidence in myself.

Remember me as I was, your admirer,
who, you may recall, followed in your steps
for several nights. In the coming days,

a deeper darkness, of course, will enclose me.
I am not afraid, Chief Minister Worm,
of a deeper darkness.

NO

Not at night, no, anyway, tomorrow,
she will not come today, today it's cold,

no, if at all, not in the dark, alone,
shadow on a wall, hand on heart, not an agitated heart,

not in fear, no, if at all, not in rain,
not when it's damp, not footsteps in the rain, not a net

of water, not a black sky, not a cloud,
not a small cloud, not now, under a green tree,

not in the street, if at all, not at the gates of the house,
not by hand, not slowly, not in the heat, under an olive
    tree,

not today, not hard, not from necessity,
not in sunlight, not in mist.

HERE THEY COME

Here they come, please look!
By the time you get here, they've gone, she said.
In the garden the worm bit deeper
into the flesh of the fruit.
It hurts! said the dog to its master.
The master ignored it. Master,
you can't imagine how it hurts.

It's only a coffin with something in it.
Nothing is left of the face.
Children ran off with the parts.

Are you searching for a path in the sea?
Do you expect to see him
awake or asleep?

As for me, I don't know.
In the eyes of others I seem a deceiver.
But as for me, I don't know.

No, I'm not searching for a path in the sea
And yes, I've been here, also I've been there.
In my opinion, the table should be moved.

The woman said she didn't like words.
I don't pass a thing on to others.

In my opinion, such matters are not reliable.

Yes, walk with me in my coming and going.
The streets are quiet, the alleys fragrant.
You may come with me.
You may also wait.
Alone, now. Later, with the music.

YOUR ATTENTION

Your attention, please! I want
to say something. He went on his way
and passed right by me. I could have touched
the hem of his coat. I didn't.
I didn't know. Neither would you have known.

Sand clung to his clothes. Bits of straw
were matted in his beard, as if he'd spent the night
in a barn. Who could have known
that in one more night he'd be
as empty as a bird, as hard as stone?

I couldn't have known. I don't blame
him. Sometimes I feel him rising
in his sleep, moonstruck, like the sea,
saying to me: Son, my son, I didn't know
how close you've been to me.

FROM YEAR TO YEAR IT

From year to year it grows more refined,
it will be so very refined in the end—
she said, speaking of it.

But sometimes I feel I'm drowning in Time,
I feel I've been drowning a long time—
he said.

It's because you're sinking, she said.
You know, it's all because you're sinking.

I don't know. Sometimes I think my strength has fled.
Refined, you know, is another word for dead.

I know and I applaud you for your discoveries.
I applaud you for your charming subtleties.
You leave nothing behind you.

But that's exactly my anxiety!
But that's exactly what will be said of me!
But that's exactly what I feel!

You're wrong again: you feel good, and goodness
    surrounds you.
Goodness, in fact, is really all around you.
Be patient, it will show its face to you.

No sooner done, it will surely embrace you.
A little time passes, its kisses will smother you.
You know how one thing leads to another.

AS THE SAND

When God in the Bible wants to promise
He points to the stars. Abraham strolls
from his tent at night
and sees lovers. As the sand
on the sea shore, the Lord says.
And man believes, even though he understands
that to say *as the sand* is merely a way
of speaking. Since that time,
sand and stars have been intertwined
in man's net of images. But perhaps
we shouldn't speak here of man.
Nothing was said of him, there and then—

and yet it is said explicitly *as the sand*,
from which we might infer
the capacity to endure. On the other hand,
it's possible to believe
that everything is then set free
and there are no more—explicitly
no more—boundaries.

As the sand on the sea shore. But then, water
is never spoken of, although
God does, explicitly, speak of seed.
which only goes to show
the ways of heaven and possibly, those
of nature, also.

SAMSON'S HAIR

I've never understood Samson's hair:
that power concealed in it, his hermetic secrecy,
the interdiction—not to be defied—
never to speak of it,
and the terrible anxiety
of being shorn, the horror each time
Delilah slips her fingers through his locks.

On the other hand
I understand quite well the hair of Absalom.
Clearly, it's beautiful, like the sun at noon,
like a red moon of vengeance,
sweeter than the many fragrances of women.
Ahithophel, sly and cunning, has to look away

when he beholds the reason for David's love.
This is the most marvelous hair
in the kingdom—which, as you can see,
explains the outbreak of each new rebellion
and later, that business with the tree.

LOVE

A boy hammers on a girl's door.
The girl doesn't open it.
The boy's head is spinning.
The girl's head is spinning.
Thousands of angels escort the sun on its way,
flying in that unique formation peculiar to angels.
Have you ever loved me? he asks.
I have, she answers, in a halting voice.

A boy hammers on a girl's door.
The girl doesn't open it.
I love you, answers the girl,
and for the first time the boy discovers
in himself true generosity.

The angels get tired. Everything made of earth
gets tired. The boy does not get tired.
A boy hammers on a girl's door.
Be astonished, O ye heavens and earth! Who knows
why a boy discovers the meaning of true generosity.

Like the mountain, says the mother. Like the mountain,
says the child, learning by rote his mother's old saw.
Like the mountain, says the boy, putting two and two together.

Who understands why the boy is hammering

on the girl's door? Who knows
why the girl doesn't open it?

I love you, whispers the girl. I love you,
repeat the stars in heaven, the pets in the house.
I love you, whispers the Angel of Death
in his pure, geometric voice.
A boy hammers on a girl's door.
How does it happen that precisely now
he learns the true meaning of generosity?

FAILURE

Seven times the wolf said to the lamb,
Beware! On the eighth he devoured it.

What brought me to want
whatever it is the heart wants?

Or led me to believe I might divide
water from water

that cannot be divided
and only in the sky

is altered to air?
Meanwhile

only the heart is still there, wishful
as ever,

and whatever was not fished up
on its hook.

TO BE THE MASTER OF YOUR HOUSE

To be the master of your house, to wrestle
against winds, to sit beneath the fig tree,

to be watchful of the foxes that spoil
the vines, to read in the book of dust,

to know the festivals of light cast down
at your feet, to be as wary of stolen water as of fire,

to touch each object twice, to sit a long time
and not look up at the clouds

passing overhead at night
on their way to the sea.

CONFESSIONS OF WAR

I've grown distant from my grandfather
while playing music. No longer do I wait
beneath the piano for his words
or listen for my name when he sings.
It seemed to me I was getting closer
and yet I'm farther.
It seemed to me he forgot,
and it is I who have forgotten.

Sometimes I asked the pilots to bring
my iron ration straight to the shelter where I hid.
I don't believe in idols; in any case,
my request wasn't granted. The war
passed over my head. They didn't know the way,
there wasn't a connection, they said.
I don't smoke American cigarettes, not even
before sleep. I don't go up in planes.
I'm not that naive.

He disappeared in fog. They say his fuel
ran out. No point in making a fuss
over what's done with. Provided, of course,
the family doesn't inquire.
The fatigue of matter—that's reason enough.
In cities grown weary of matter
naphthalene lamentations drift in colored darkness

like an alchemic liquid from the Middle Ages.
The meticulous gentleman of my own age
is counting worn coins—worthless,
without future, and unearthed, layer by layer—
late dust witnessed by a dimmed, final vision.

Hands trembling, the antiquary unfurls
the scroll of genealogy, nullified long ago.
In an un-theatrical light of the sun
his hairy hands seem immense. Monsters, by comparison,
are microbes distorted by water. Mountains
are only places to come down from. Airplanes are bees
that stopped buzzing. They gather bombs, not honey,
with hands, not wings, hazarding dust and sleep.
Deceit lights its fires on the hills to signal
one more conclusion. And balding amnesiacs
huddle together in debate,
pointing to maps that even yesterday
had nothing to hide beneath the sand.

SERGEANT WEISS

On your forehead now
the everlasting flower.
Invisible worms
are nourished at your cheeks.
On maneuvers your name
is seldom mentioned. Your flesh
is like a sieve: you leave
and enter as you wish. But your hand,
with a watch that marks the earth's time,
still troubles my hours.
Before you came I had believed it necessary
to hurry to my task.

I don't know what you think of children these days.
It's even difficult to picture
your face in the moment of horror.
It seems that events
have already moved on
as to a late reel of film, beyond recall.
But in the desert they still worship you
in soldiers' boots. The bramble
remembers the sound of your commands
and bows.

Sergeant Weiss, I don't know how much time will pass
before I suddenly remember you,

restless again.
Perhaps you were right. You built your house
where you can't be reached except by cold, heat, hunger,
desire perhaps. Water will not well around your eyes,
the oleander will not sing in your tongue.
Your mother is dead, Sergeant Weiss.
You will not be a child again.
In this eternal parody of men's fates
war takes one of the leading parts.
Styled by the inarticulate, it never knows
its image: it engulfs you like a sea
that bores through the swimmer's flesh
and rushes on—to death, victory—headlong,
heedless of all but motion.
Your madness is one possibility,
not the worst. You, at least, create a condition
we can't appeal.
But at the heart of these illusions that vanish
and leave nothing behind to show
they existed, I sometimes see
your amazed eyes, like oases
that aren't mine. We who were unable, all these years,
to shape war into something we can grasp
remember you as a closely written page—illegible,
perhaps, but correct, setting down the days that passed
and were not fulfilled.

HOW THE DAYS PASSED

1

How the days passed! Who would have thought
they pass like this. How time passes, and the sky,
even the wind!

The wind whirled once in the tree, abhoring our
memories.
You who were once mine
do not belong now
even to the stars.

2

Under the fallen leaves autumn lay waiting
for its time, secret as the locust.
Slowly, so very slowly, the body's rain falls,
the terrifying hair withers.

A piece of driftwood on the shore
draws comfort from the wind.

Fish slide away from the surface
in a heavy murmur. Young forever,
their eyes are petrified water.

The place they will set aside for us
one day in another place
is preparing itself:
the earth never tires of being opened.

Already I hear the riders galloping
on the plain. Mother! the boy cried, I can see
their iron hooves! Hush, said the mother. Hush,
child I bore, child I gave the world,
you see nothing.

When will the wondrous diamonds blossom
from the coal of my eyes? When will I see you again
and hold you, and my lips
whisper of love?

I do not know. To be precise: I do not know.
What I had, I tried to give. Such matters
are long and weary. This isn't the place to speak of them.
They didn't change the world.
It's the salt in me that talks.

3

He doesn't know;
he's never known, they told the examiner.
Now that he's told us
everything he knows,
it's clear he doesn't know.
It's quite clear he isn't lying.
I know, said the examiner.
There are some things I know,
and some things I remember.
That's how I am. That's me.

WHEN THE LAST RIDERS

When the last riders disappear over the horizon
and even the dust of their horses no longer rises
I'll know it is time to lock the gate.
The spent day will close its hands and be content.
For me the hour will be familiar. Come now,
I'll tell myself, it isn't the first time
you've seen them come and go.
The sun, of course, will be indifferent to my words.
Blood red, it will go down behind the mountains
as if I were bereft in the world. There is no other sun.
The creator puts aside his handiwork,
the angels' verdict is in the locked book.

The gate must be closed, logic tells me. At night
the dark is darkest.

THE MAN IN WHITE

The man in white
walked with sureness
in the night

And I followed him with hard eyes
step by step
as he passed by

And I understood that for me
there is no whiteness
in the night

And no light that can erase
even my farthest grief
that lies in wait

But also there is no single light
that can close the gate
a man in white

opens in the night

THE QUIET LIGHT OF FLIES

The quiet light of flies
sinks. The desert answers
with a faint drum of hooves.

Silk scarves
sway from the spines of cactus,
and in the silvery tents
they are dancing the Dance of Jars.

Springs well up,
springs with their white stones,
springs with their musty deaths—
one bucket,
another,
and another,
they shiver in the wind like hanged men

and still there's time to rest,
the night drifts.

NOT EVERYTHING

And still I've not said everything
I still have more to say

before the hour grows late and the crowd scatters
and each remembers then

what a man remembers when others are done
saying what they said and what they haven't said

and still I've not said everything

from ALL THE MILK AND THE HONEY
(1964)

WORDS

Such joy, such pain, these are only words.
Conceal your joy. Gather your pain
into a safe place. Write only when your hand
needs nothing, not even the loose change
of the world. That which is crooked
cannot be made straight.
Don't go on straightening it.

Such joy, such pain, people say.
What they mean is themselves.
Lie in wait; surprise yourself
in secrecy, in blood: when such joy appears,
such pain, tell yourself that a man
is not suited for such joy,
such pain forever, has no right
to strut them out on stage, no right
with such joy, such pain
to wound himself,
not to speak of others. Such joy,
such pain—didn't you know?—
they come and go.

GREATER COURAGE

The courage to wait
is greater than the courage to confess.
With pain it's easier to gain the sympathy
of others, which is not the case
with waiting.

You are alone here. You hang a picture
on the wall, straighten a rug, listen to footsteps pass,
think that you're miserable but remind yourself
you are not unique. Yet carefully
you tear a letter into shreds.
Here you are wholly on your own. Judge yourself,
if you must. But remember: this, too,
is not what matters.

AND PERHAPS ONLY MUSIC

And perhaps only music. Since the emotion
is obscure, call it what you wish.
Only music, perhaps. Here it is
of an evening, hesitant
in the absence of strong feeling,
uncertain. So David, in his day,
must have played. But Saul didn't suspect.
Manly and confident, he hurled his spear
as if in David's song there stood forth
matters final and clear-cut
like the severed head of Goliath.

SOMETIMES LATE AT NIGHT

Sometimes late at night
I sit at the piano and play. What does one need?
How little one needs to be sustained,

even here, not to speak of better worlds
in the future. Indeed,
how little. My skilled hands glide across the keys

and I play. Ah, if only I could play! Yet even this
is enough. I'm not like Saul with his envy.
How little one needs: the nightly calm descends, and

one almost can believe life is redeemed, that it's possible
to live even here, this spring, without
the whole cast of Genesis: God,

tree, apple, Eve, the serpent.

THIS SLOW UNEARTHLY SPELL
for Peter and Shulamit

This slow, unearthly spell of standing still.
Not to trade places with, or envy
those flying overhead at night, passing
in a shriek of polished and cold metal,
jostling each other in a mysterious light.

Not to set out again and again. To spend each evening
among familiar tokens, making
a barren speech before the stars. Keeping close watch
over Time's steps. To bring to an end
all that is loved and rare
with an unhurried hand and a shattered heart.

THREE POEMS

1

I could cross the border
but I don't want to.

Besides, the evenings now
are cool and blue.

If I buy a fancy blue suit
and wear it into the street
I might stand out.

But I'll feel odd.

2

The birds are distant now
and twitter in other trees.
In the air, hints of September.

I'd like to travel
if only I knew where.

I'd like to find a woman with a plait
who'll be content with this closet,

and if she isn't—
I'll buy us a large and spacious flat.
Four rooms.

3

A friend returned
from a long journey.
I look into his eyes.

There's no denying
something clings to him—
salt water or the sparkle of diamonds.

He speaks and I see
his pupils dilating:
The world is wide, life sweet.

I ask him what are his plans now.
What a question! He'll buy a hammer
and make the crooked straight.

SOMETIMES

Sometimes I leave the room and phone myself.
I watch to see who's coming and am amazed.
I didn't know I'd been standing there so long.

The one for whom I waited didn't come. I'm writing him
a letter. It's the end of winter, I write, even the potted plants
on the roof show signs of spring. When Honorable Sir comes,
I add, I'll prepare a celebration.

Meanwhile, the winds remain cool. The noonday noise of the city
drowns out the noise of the sea. Flocks of hoarse blackbirds are
    calling.
Now they sleep. Trees are black shapes. It's cool.

I'd like to say something to Honorable Sir, something
extraordinary that I've never said. I search the table
with my hand, bump against the matches again. I go on writing.
Goes and turns about all this, what?! goes and turns about.

AGAINST PARTING

My tailor is against parting.
That's why, he
said, he's not going away;
he doesn't want to part
from his only daughter. He's definitely
against parting.

Once, he parted from his wife
and he never did see her
after this (Auschwitz).
Parted
from his three sisters and
these he never again
looked upon (Buchenwald).
He once parted from his mother (his father
died at a ripe old age). Now
he's against parting.

In Berlin he was
my father's close companion. They passed
a good time in
that Berlin. The time passed. Now
he'll never travel. He's
most definitely
(my father died meanwhile)
against parting.

ORPHEUS

Orpheus walks this evening
in the footprints of Eurydice (the path is strewn

with pine needles). My lady, I am
leaving. My lady, I do not turn

my head to see the view,
neither to look at you. Lady,

do not be angry. I have with me
my violin, I can play to shorten

the journey. Approximately
at the third turn, hell became too beautiful:

red birds were glowing like sparks
in the burnt trees, early flowers

of an early blossoming. The vision of Eurydice's
soft nape. Always her nape. Oh, here comes

Springtime! says sly Orpheus
to his blundering heart:

To look back once, just
once. —The hand,

of its own volition,
is already arching over the violin.

ORPHEUS LAMENTS

Orpheus laments tonight. Why all this uproar?
Orpheus laments. He refuses
to be consoled. At twilight he hung his violin
on a tree. Now he laments.

No, he won't be consoled.
Some heartless thief, in the dark, stole
his violin when he was gone.
Orpheus is lamenting tonight. Listen!
The moon's gone dumb, birds
cease their singing, the wind doesn't sigh
in the tree, the river froze
in its bed. The voice travels far,
far into the distance. Who's howling out there?

Who's inconsolable? Who's making
that racket? Who disturbs
the peace?

BE ATTENTIVE

Be attentive to this trembling shade.
Stretch out your hand to feel the wind, touch
carefully this tree. It's green, and greener still
at the crown, the trunk
a little bitten, though it still drinks deeply
from the earth which no one sees
in the city.
Be attentive, feel, touch carefully. Breathe in
the light, harder. Illuminate
each cloud. It's passing. And night
won't wait.

A SHORT WINTER TALE

The apprentice in the shop across from me
—blacksmith or carpenter—
had a girl.
Each day at the close of work
(I end my work at eight,
then take a short walk)
I'd see her sitting on a stool
in her woolen cap, swinging her leg
to some popular tune
while the boy finished-up his work,

an hour late, as usual.
Now the girl is gone, and I don't know
who or what takes place at the blacksmith's
or carpenter's shop. But I know this:
winter passed and spring nights ooze like honey
from the lamp. And one must find, without delay,
rest equal to each pain, grief
in measure for the lover,
peace ample enough for those who sit late
keeping the hour.

And for this, time is brief,
the task is great.

ALMOST HERE

It's not true, I tell myself;
it doesn't have to be so. It can be otherwise.
There were also other nights, kept safe
in memory.

So forget what frightened you, just now, in bed
and made you get up and light the lamp:
3 a.m. The woman of pearls and coal-black hair
is no farther tonight
than on all other nights.
She is almost here.

IN THIS DEEP DARKNESS

In this deep, fumbling darkness
remember me who stood before you
thirty-two years, to the day,
in this deep, fumbling darkness.

Remember me when you climb the watchtower
at dusk in a red spray of light.
Remember me when you drive away stray clouds
from this world to another

where clouds are forgotten.
Remember me among all your flocks
more than you have remembered all your orphans
in this deep, fumbling darkness

where I am lost more than an orphan,
more than a lamb, for my eyes
are open, I can see how blue darkens, I am not
deceived, I see how blood thickens,

the voice falters, how everything returns
at evening to remind us and to speak for all
that has ever been, all that is changeless, homeless
in this deep, fumbling darkness.

A SONG TO MAKE PEACE

A song to make peace.
On such an evening, God, as this,
that falls like a truce, if sometimes I could also sing
a song to make peace, implore you
to shine the light of your countenance
upon all your worms, crawling
wherever they are, loved
and unloved, appeased
and unappeased, God
and unGod.

THE BIRD

I saw a bird of rare beauty.
The bird looked at me.
In all the days of my life
never again will I see
such a beautiful bird.

A shiver of light went through me.
I said words of peace.
Words I spoke yesterday,
today I will not speak.

from NORTH EASTERLY
(1979)

THE PROBLEM

1

The problem, of course, is to shape a form
like a diamond, but also like an ample bed
where a man can stretch without
knocking his head against a wall,
and like a taut string
with no corners to catch dust.

2

What you are meant to say
you say with suspicious fluency.
What you wish to say
sometimes is said between the lines.
But what you make an effort to say
is not said, as if it were so meant.

3

And once again the evening sky—vast emptiness
in which clouds, planes are scribbling tiny streaks and curls.
They are the dynamic element: what is written and then
        erased.

And autumn confuses in you the ripe, plaintive fruit
that asks only to stop, to delay, to fix
each brilliance in the opening of the black gullet.
And this is impossible. For this there is no time.

4

The poet's time is always
too long or too short, like shoes
that pinch or slip.
What you wish to say to future generations
must be said now, but you keep busy
rummaging through drawers.
Perhaps it's better this way: last year's rain
no one but you remembers,
and words to your grandchildren
will not return to be revised and weighed.
Here, cunning is required. This is the static element:
to speak to the moment, like a journalist,
and hope it will stretch a little
or as much as possible.

A STRANGER WON'T UNDERSTAND

A day of unplanned sunlight. A sea gull flares
above the roof, an open parachute.
Here is the sudden turn I too
should have been able to make.
At my age it's difficult.
But I tell myself: I'll try.
Without strain, however. The secret of beauty lies
in the effortless. A graceful thing
doesn't beat its wings—it sails,
floats, hovers
beyond the reach of antennas, iron combs
digging out bits of cant from the air.
A stranger won't understand how hard
it is for the ordinary newspaper reader,
or the man standing in line, to unfurl
his wings,
let alone do a proper job of anything.
To flap one's mouth, now and then,
is something else
entirely.

ON THE IMPOSSIBILITY OF THE
UNROMANTIC CONDITION

A starry night at last Van Gogh
in the café unabashed
whirling about like the moon in orbit
like stars
skimming the newspaper lit-up in mirrors drinking
not that I haven't heard
the sound of running water
but I said to myself the tap
there were extenuating circumstances
I am not a prophet nor the son of one
I was even wearing the slippers I carry with me
ready for nightmares such as this
on a wild night, a sleepless night.
How many canvases were abandoned and all
that was driven away returns as if summoned:
on a sidewalk at a local café
a man sits and hears his name—
Yes, I am aware. Yes, I recollect.
At last an unequivocal answer.
A starry night?
No. Not yet.

NOTHING TO SHOUT ABOUT

Everything begins with the morning shave,
ends with lights out at one or two.
Thus the daily order
can become a terrible disorder in the dark.

Not younger and not much older.
No need to complain yet, considering the years.
The beard is short and non-prophetic,
the glance exact and almost clinical
(the doctor trembling in the mirror is me).

The body doesn't hurt yet, but it's already a burden.
The belly sags, you learn to live with it.
The forces that once leapt free from the cage
return to it as destructive forces.

Thus and forthwith and so on and hence—
What's new? Nothing under the sun.
And whoever looks to a bad end
has not learned from bitter experience.

TO RISE FROM ASHES

is a complicated business. Only one bird is an expert,
and even it, apparently, is never seen.
The first condition, of course, is ash: embers,
dead ashes, the ash of cigarettes,
almost anything. In the absence of ash,
broken-ends will do, plaster debris, a total collapse,
ruins. Whatever is anti-biological, anti-ecological.
A further condition is the ability to rise
and stand on your feet after the fall,
a condition also found in the boxing ring:
the odds are against you, you're in the late rounds,
even your fans have turned away thinking
of home and supper.
When younger, I knew a man—an expert, certainly!—who rose
each Monday from the weekend's ashes
and each Friday from the week's ashes. Only a handful
of men are like this: a sort of resurrection artist,
akin to Kafka's hunger artist.
But for everyone who rose I met a number who didn't.
Some burned in a small fire, ordinary,
like the flame of a kerosene stove;
and some went up in a sudden blaze, like dry thorns,
accompanied by sirens and bells.
And in this men are no different than women,
the young no different than the old,
each person has his appointed hour.

And one occupation is like another—workers blaze up!
Exactly like clerks and those in the liberal professions,
despite the rumor they're more fireproof.
Only a few of these will rise again
and stand. One needn't despair at this. On the contrary,
your common birdwatcher will swear to it: the phoenix
is not a mythological creature. It's here among us,
but it's rare.

ANOTHER CITY
for Amnon and Daneilla

Graham Greene in his elegant style:
"My roots are in the absence of roots."
Later, a style better suited for a tiresome task—
even in a train to Istanbul
it's possible to grow sick of writing,
more so in South America.
A man flies his typewriter
to five continents like someone
stepping out to relieve his dog
or spite the neighbors.

Squares of light in the plane window.
A seatbelt—to make certain nothing will burst forward
and the unexpected happen.
We have the freedom of choice,
but our choice is so limited:
a meat or vegetarian menu.

At the hotel the grave-faced concierge:
The first shall be the last...something like that.
But the suitcase grows lighter
after the tip.
And so, looking back, you see it was all worthwhile—
you could be born, God forbid! a politician
or not be born at all.

There remains then the worries of making a living.
A man needs a smile, a good word and a loan.
The rest needn't be mentioned.
The words photograph a given situation:
A body leaning against the headboard, glancing around
    the room,
—Not bad,
another city that tells it nothing.

THE CITY

Closing your eyes won't help. Who can condemn
the perfectly cunning bomb, the mine placed just so,
without some slight hope for change—like pointing
to an abscess or like a doctor
writing another dose for the dying.

Leave the world in men's hands and watch
what happens: a mob of predators
tearing at other predators—some small—
in butcher shops and highways,
in bedrooms and voting booths.

Leave a city in the hands of architects,
contractors, city council:
yesterday, skyscrapers to plumb
the heavens. Today, hives
and cattle pens, holes stuffed with mortgages and loans,
squares circled dizzily by traffic.

And yet, always, there is this city:
you arrive near evening,
always on time, as scheduled,
happy with the white sheets on the bed,
and open the suitcase
and remove a book and glasses
and turn on the radio and forgive

whoever hung the mirror and the reproductions
and arrange a few notes for a talk
and remember a face or a photograph
and walk downstairs to survey the hotel bar
when the window fills with darkness
and tiny lights begin blossoming
in a city that's foreign and lovely
and yes, night falls
and it's yours.

CARVED IN STONE

As years go by,
the original plan is disrupted.

What was carved in stone keeps being erased,
as if line and relief returned to the bosom of stone.

Marble becomes water-stained, the color of brick
is damaged, everything drips or washes away.

A shoe sinks in the canal
where only branches float.

The wooden stars on the lintel stream away,
the house-frame leans like a tree over water.

What was once cut in acute angles
rounds itself again and curls—like ripple

and net in the current, waves moving
with wind, waves folding over waves

when a boat passes. What is built on the sea
longs to be sea again. A window

throws its momentary patch of colored dye
into the water. It's dangerous to open a window.

There is no stone without its hour; there is no hour
that didn't carve in stone as a sediment
growing like marsh grass and seaweed.

TWILIGHT

Twilight, to be ready, practices
with a line and a steady hand—like a tattoo—

engraving the fixed times for loss;
the evening is honed to a skin

until it's fine, until it's sensitized, as if its end
is to be a film of glass transparent to its pain.

To be a stone is the dream of everyone.
But in the dream everyone carries a stone

and water covers the dream
and light wraps the face of the water

with a slack hard hand, hard slack
as if it made everything equal for now.

Amsterdam, December 1967

IN NIGHT'S REALM

In night's realm the red hood
was torn from her head—
monster ancient as night
blind in the scalding mirror.

The tree at the window sill
whispers to itself.
The veteran wolf is haggling:
Grandmother or girl?

Up in the thick sky floats
a red hood.
Red blood at its feet,
blood of a slaughtered wolf.

FOG

Fog over the morning's face.
Particles of fog turn into particles of light—
light equally sown, gathered
into the sun's pale circle,

as if it renewed the green of an invisible meadow
which will then shine forth
deeper green, dripping with water.
This is the face of a land
that bears over and over again—

so much, it becomes alien.
Who'd dare recall a desert here?
In the prayer book in church even the desert
seems green, nestled in shadow.
It's easy to identify with your own,
and to you was given a wilderness unsown

and a light consumed
by promises and dreams: kine
and ears of corn and sheaves.
In the meantime
seven lean years, and after them
seven more, least you forget. And in a short while
the cycle will be complete.
Thus time moves on, it destroys.

Here, time barely moves. In this fog
that tells you nothing of warmth
or tenderness or grief, among signs
that have never touched you,
apparently you grow. But a stranger's hand
gathered the harvest. What remains

is the memory of a broken mirror, an inward
habit, and a little green that enters
your eyes, in spite of itself— here and there,
blossoming.

Colchester, 1968

STILL LIFE

A young man leans from the window to gape
at the twilight, his body half-way out
in a redundant gesture.

A light breeze trembles the scenic view of the water.
An impressionistic man in anxious gray
breaks off, for his private needs, a crooked piece

of the evening as a sign for pain.
A woman who wanted to enter the picture
hesitates at the edge of the still life.

The man has not yet finished his work.
The woman is not his wife.

There are no more details.

DAY

First day, month of June. Like a ship's captain
I make an entry: the river quiet, no fish, no fisherman.

Not a breath of wind, each leaf
hangs motionless, the mottled foliage

freezes in place— far shades graying a little,
near ones showing green.

"A bird shot into the sky."
It's only twilight. This also is not freedom.

WIND

The wind brings peace to what was. To what never was,
wind does not bring peace. To one's surprise, this too
is a place: the poet brings it forth
with the breath of his mouth,
the writing of his eyes— an old ruse.
When I say you, already you smile. When I glance at my watch
you grow unhappy. Pretty girl, how little
you require, and what little profit there is in love.
This place is worse than hell:
hell is, is real.

THE STORK DANCES

The boat rocked in the waves
its gunwale knocking against the pier
a firefly melted small points of fire
in the water
somewhere a dark metallic glint
of fish streaming in the undercurrents
beside a tree that lowered
its tide of branches to the water
marking an ephemeral fact we sat
and spoke easily of things
plain matters and matters that circled about themselves
a world adequate to itself and to me
you leaned your head back against your purse
you were telling the family tale
are you cold?
peals of laughter from the inn
at night laughter seems strained and unreal
a pretty profile
intense
a pale hunter turning gray

PLOT

I pored and pored over the text to find
where she entered and who had a hand in it.
An amateur detective, I found
only footprints.

At the beach two bodies
joined on the sand, abandoned car,
typewriter— enough for a typical
lethal plot. The radio playing.

Once it was risky.
Nude photos in the drawer.
A small box, empty and yellowing.
A pair of nylons. In September or December.
I'm writing this down from memory.
Up to this point everything is clear.

Having no way out, words join
in a small, compulsive rhythm. The foot taps it.
The ritual varies from country to country
but keeps its own logic:
once every year.

Alone, slowly, the knife blade dances,
works the abstractions, strips away,
veil after veil falls: I'm not

the first. I slept
beside her almost a year.
So what.

AS THE YEARS PASS

As the years pass, the magus grows withdrawn and weak;
the rare that was a daily presence
dwindles into an unexpected guest.
The rest of the time you read the world
in the news and the palm of your hand.

What was taken for granted became
a kind of revelation.
The constant search, so little to be desired,
became itself the end:
half the sky is in the light of a dying day,
half threatening a storm—

once more a sign is given of days
burning anew in our riddled flesh,
the miracle restored.
Thus towns and countries go rushing by

in the train window, an unreliable
interpreter. But you stop
in the twilight of a winter's evening, here
in this darkening city, before sleep,
to witness again the secret.

A GUST OF WARM WIND

Summer, and the land stirring— a gust of warm wind
and camels in the street, a swarm of bees
lifting in smoke. The remnant of the Canaanites
is spilling into the streets.

These are the waters that wear down the stones
and deepen the hidden cleft of the well. In the Book,
Rachel still goes down with her jar, the moon rises
and gnaws holes in the darkness.

The old frenzy in the blood
still stones the living. And a harsh hand
soothes the forehead with a damp rag,
promising the sick man in his bed

that truly his night shall be sweet.
There is something in promises—
remote, a secret wrapped in desires
no one can unravel—

the wadi winding its way,
the city that rose from salt,
the strange end of Job:
forms of things to come.

LANDSCAPES

In familiar landscapes
I get lost in what is unclear to me.
The linen wick dipped in oil
refuses to burn.
Not that I suddenly grew weary,
but the old familiar fatigue keeps
nailing me to rocks and salt.
When evening comes, once again
the armies of the uprooted
march in my blood.
Even though I kept so distant,
more than Vogel perhaps,
there's something despotic
in this closeness:
that I managed to slip away
I almost picture myself as a victim.

A FAREWELL SONG

The old man holding the oar,
the man in shadows, the miller,
the couple making love in the barn
confirm the distant rumor of life
spoken of in rumors.
Night after night they stand near us,
spirits captive of their past—
once they resembled us
and could, if they so desired, sing.
Look! A youthful evening is falling
and they all return, the old with the young.
Oh, there's never an end to sorrow,
also there is no sorrow in the world.
Frozen like figures of wax
far from the honey we gathered,
they turn our lives, as well,
in their own way to honey.
So open your window to the evening
and let the wind-shapes enter—
the old man holding the oar,
the man in shadows, the miller,
the couple crying out in the night—
to testify that nothing is lost here
and that nothing is here but what is lost
and that all their wants are laid upon us
and they rest in peace at last.

THE COUNTRIES WE LIVE IN

The countries we live in
are ambiguous
and extend in different directions,
far off into the vistas
beneath the balcony.
These flickering lights
are also typical lights—
landscapes, elements,
their end: to go on. Their end: to go out.
The sun also rises and the sun goes down
following its path to the sea
through the narrow corridor set aside for it.
From east to the uttermost end of west
there is no new shadow
and the order of things is good—
also, there is no other order.
Here is tranquility and peace at day's end
for a tired body and a spirit
sick of itself, rebellious—
this also is true. And a bird
filling with blood
is a falling bird, a rising bird,
better than these, a small bird in the hand
—Look! How soft its down,
a blackbird, its color lovely to behold.
And the other two have flown.

NOTES

from EARLY POEMS

"The Gold of Ophir"
Ophir is the legendary biblical city of great riches. Solomon is said to have received a portion of his wealth from there.

"To a Student in Jerusalem"
Hamsin is the Arabic word for a hot, dry, oppressive wind that arrives from the inland desert, reputed to create psychological or emotional difficulties in some people.

"I Saw a White Bird"
"a cloud as small as a man's hand": 1 Kings 18-44. The servant of the prophet Elijah reports seeing such a cloud on his seventh ascent of Mount Carmel. Elijah takes this as a sign of his mission. As the rain arrives, he travels with Ahab to Jezreel.

"Also"
The closing couplet of the poem alludes to a curse placed upon those who fail to enter the covenant made with God. See Deuteronomy 29: 17-18.

from VARIOUS POEMS

"Chief Minister Worm"
"half my desire in hand": idiomatic, meaning that one shouldn't go to the grave with desires only half fulfilled.

"As The Sand"
The story is told in Genesis 22:17. Zach parodies a rabbinical exegesis of the text.

"Samson's Hair"
2 Samuel 18:6: Absalom leads a rebellion against his father, King David. In the Battle of Ephraim Wood, his hair is entangled in the branches of an oak tree when he rides beneath them. Helpless, he is killed by Joab.

from ALL THE MILK AND THE HONEY

"And Perhaps Only Music"
For the incident involving Saul and David, see 1 Samuel 18:6-12.

"Three Poems"
Ecclesiastes 1:15: "That which is crooked cannot be made straight, and that which is wanting cannot be numbered."

"Sometimes"
Ecclesiastes 1:6: "The wind goes toward the south, and turns about unto the north; it whirls about continually, and the wind returns again according to its circuits."

from NORTH EASTERLY

"Landscapes"
David Vogel (1891-1943): Hebrew poet, born in Podolia, wandered through Eastern and Western Europe during World War I and II. He briefly visited Palestine but returned to France, where he was captured by the Nazis and killed in a concentration camp.

"The Countries We Live In"
"The sun also rises and the sun goes down": Ecclesiastes 1:5.

ABOUT THE TRANSLATOR

PETER EVERWINE was born in Detroit and grew up in Western Pennsylvania. His most recent collections are *From the Meadow: Selected and New Poems* and *Working the Song Fields*, a translation of Aztec poems. He is the recipient of an American Academy of Arts and Letters Award in Literature, and fellowships from the National Endowment for the Arts and the John Simon Guggenheim Foundation.

ABOUT TAVERN BOOKS

Tavern Books is an independent publisher of poetry based in Portland, Oregon, and Salt Lake City, Utah. In addition to reviving books that have fallen out of print, we seek to build a catalog of poetry in translation from the finest writers of our modern era. We edit and publish this series based on the philosophy that works of vision deserve inclusion in a living library. We believe that the essential books of our time should be in print and made available to the reading public in beautiful, lasting editions.

BOOKS IN THIS SERIES

Casual Ties by David Wevill

The Boy Changed into a Stag Clamors at the Gate of Secrets
by Ferenc Juhász,
translated from the Hungarian by David Wevill

Under an Arkansas Sky by Jo McDougall

Arthur's Talk with the Eagle by Anonymous,
translated from the Welsh by Gwyneth Lewis

Twelve Poems about Cavafy by Yannis Ritsos,
translated from the Greek by Paul Merchant

Night of Shooting Stars by Leonardo Sinisgalli,
translated from the Italian by W. S. Di Piero

Prodigy by Charles Simic,
drawings by Charles Seluzicki

Ocean by Joseph Millar

The Countries We Live In by Natan Zach,
translated from the Hebrew by Peter Everwine

Notes on Sea & Shore by Greta Wrolstad

Dhaka City by Zubair Ahmed

My Blue Piano by Else Lasker-Schüler,
translated from the German by Eavan Boland

Buson: Haiku by Yosa Buson,
translated from the Japanese by Franz Wright

COLOPHON

This book was designed and typeset by Michael McGriff. The text is set in Garamond, an old-style serif typeface named for the punch-cutter Claude Garamond (c. 1480 – 1561). The titles are set in Myriad, a humanist sans-serif typeface designed by Robert Slimbach and Carol Twombly. Printed on archival-quality paper at McNaughton & Gunn, Inc.

In this edition, twenty-six copies are signed and lettered A – Z by the translator.